D0537697

by Iain Gray

WRITING *to* REMEMBER

LangSyne
PUBLISHING
WRITING *to* REMEMBER

Strathclyde Business Centre
120 Carstairs Street, Glasgow G40 4JD
Tel: 0141 554 9944 Fax: 0141 554 9955
E-mail: info@scottish-memories.co.uk
www.langsyneshop.co.uk

Design by Dorothy Meikle
Printed by Thomson Litho, East Kilbride
© Lang Syne Publishers Ltd 2008

ISBN 1-85217-299-1

Clancy

MOTTO:
Fidelity and fortitude.

CREST:
A hand holding a sword
impaling a boar's head.

NAME variations include:
MacFhlannchaidh *(Gaelic)*,
Magfhlannchadha *(Gaelic)*,
Clancey, Clanchey, Clanchy,
Clansey, Glancy, MacClancy.

Chapter one:

Origins of Irish surnames

**According to an old saying, there are two types of Irish –
those who actually are Irish and those who wish they were.**

This sentiment is only one example of the allure that the
high romance and drama of the proud nation's history holds
for thousands of people scattered across the world today.

It's a sad fact, however, that the vast majority of Irish
surnames are found far beyond Irish shores, rather than on
the Emerald Isle itself.

The population stood at around eight million souls in
1841, but today it stands at fewer than six million.

This is mainly a tragic consequence of the potato
famine, also known as the Great Hunger, which devastated
Ireland between 1845 and 1849.

The Irish peasantry had become almost wholly reliant
for basic sustenance on the potato, first introduced from the
Americas in the seventeenth century.

When the crop was hit by a blight, at least 800,000
people starved to death while an estimated two million
others were forced to seek a new life far from their native
shores – particularly in America, Canada, and Australia.

The effects of the potato blight continued until about
1851, by which time a firm pattern of emigration had
become established.

Ireland's loss, however, was to the gain of the countries in which the immigrants settled, contributing enormously, as their descendants do today, to the well being of the nations in which their forefathers settled.

But those who were forced through dire circumstance to establish a new life in foreign parts never forgot their roots, or the proud heritage and traditions of the land that gave them birth.

Nor do their descendants.

It is a heritage that is inextricably bound up in the colourful variety of Irish names themselves – and the origin and history of these names forms an integral part of the vibrant drama that is the nation's history, one of both glorious fortune and tragic misfortune.

This history is well documented, and one of the most important and fascinating of the earliest sources are *The Annals of the Four Masters*, compiled between 1632 and 1636 by four friars at the Franciscan Monastery in County Donegal.

Compiled from earlier sources, and purporting to go back to the Biblical Deluge, much of the material takes in the mythological origins and history of Ireland and the Irish.

This includes tales of successive waves of invaders and settlers such as the Fomorians, the Partholonians, the Nemedians, the Fir Bolgs, the Tuatha De Danann, and the Laigain.

Of particular interest are the *Milesian Genealogies*,

because the majority of Irish clans today claim a descent from either Heremon, Ir, or Heber – three of the sons of Milesius, a king of what is now modern day Spain.

These sons invaded Ireland in the second millennium B.C, apparently in fulfilment of a mysterious prophecy received by their father.

This Milesian lineage is said to have ruled Ireland for nearly 3,000 years, until the island came under the sway of England's King Henry II in 1171 following what is known as the Cambro-Norman invasion.

This is an important date not only in Irish history in general, but for the effect the invasion subsequently had for Irish surnames.

'Cambro' comes from the Welsh, and 'Cambro-Norman' describes those Welsh knights of Norman origin who invaded Ireland.

But they were invaders who stayed, inter-marrying with the native Irish population and founding their own proud dynasties that bore Cambro-Norman names such as Archer, Barbour, Brannagh, Fitzgerald, Fitzgibbon, Fleming, Joyce, Plunkett, and Walsh – to name only a few.

These 'Cambro-Norman' surnames that still flourish throughout the world today form one of the three main categories in which Irish names can be placed – those of Gaelic-Irish, Cambro-Norman, and Anglo-Irish.

Previous to the Cambro-Norman invasion of the twelfth century, and throughout the earlier invasions and settlement of those wild bands of sea rovers known as the Vikings in the eighth and ninth centuries, the population of the island was relatively small, and it was normal for a person to be identified through the use of only a forename.

But as population gradually increased and there were many more people with the same forename, surnames were adopted to distinguish one person, or one community, from another.

Individuals identified themselves with their own particular tribe, or 'tuath', and this tribe – that also became known as a clann, or clan – took its name from some distinguished ancestor who had founded the clan.

The Gaelic-Irish form of the name Kelly, for example, is Ó Ceallaigh, or O'Kelly, indicating descent from an original 'Ceallaigh', with the 'O' denoting 'grandson of.' The name was later anglicised to Kelly.

The prefix 'Mac' or 'Mc', meanwhile, as with the clans of the Scottish Highlands, denotes 'son of.'

Although the Irish clans had much in common with their Scottish counterparts, one important difference lies in what are known as 'septs', or branches, of the clan.

Septs of Scottish clans were groups who often bore an entirely different name from the clan name but were under the clan's protection.

In Ireland, septs were groups that shared the same name and who could be found scattered throughout the four provinces of Ulster, Leinster, Munster, and Connacht.

The 'golden age' of the Gaelic-Irish clans, infused as their veins were with the blood of Celts, pre-dates the Viking invasions of the eighth and ninth centuries and the Norman invasion of the twelfth century, and the sacred heart of the country was the Hill of Tara, near the River Boyne, in County Meath.

Known in Gaelic as 'Teamhar na Rí', or Hill of Kings, it was the royal seat of the 'Ard Rí Éireann', or High King of Ireland, to whom the petty kings, or chieftains, from the island's provinces were ultimately subordinate.

It was on the Hill of Tara, beside a stone pillar known as the Irish 'Lia Fáil', or Stone of Destiny, that the High Kings were inaugurated and, according to legend, this stone would emit a piercing screech that could be heard all over Ireland when touched by the hand of the rightful king.

The Hill of Tara is today one of the island's main tourist attractions.

Opposition to English rule over Ireland, established in the wake of the Cambro-Norman invasion, broke out frequently and the harsh solution adopted by the powerful forces of the Crown was to forcibly evict the native Irish from their lands.

These lands were then granted to Protestant colonists, or 'planters', from Britain.

Many of these colonists, ironically, came from Scotland and were the descendants of the original 'Scotti', or 'Scots', who gave their name to Scotland after migrating there in the fifth century A.D., from the north of Ireland.

Colonisation entailed harsh penal laws being imposed on the majority of the native Irish population, stripping them practically of all of their rights.

The Crown's main bastion in Ireland was Dublin and its environs, known as the Pale, and it was the dispossessed peasantry who lived outside this Pale, desperately striving to eke out a meagre living.

It was this that gave rise to the modern-day expression of someone or something being 'beyond the pale'.

Attempts were made to stamp out all aspects of the ancient Gaelic-Irish culture, to the extent that even to bear a Gaelic-Irish name was to invite discrimination.

This is why many Gaelic-Irish names were anglicised with, for example, and noted above, Ó Ceallaigh, or O'Kelly, being anglicised to Kelly.

Succeeding centuries have seen strong revivals of Gaelic-Irish consciousness, however, and this has led to many families reverting back to the original form of their name, while the language itself is frequently found on the fluent tongues of an estimated 90,000 to 145,000 of the island's population.

Ireland's turbulent history of religious and political strife is one that lasted well into the twentieth century, a landmark century that saw the partition of the island into the twenty-six counties of the independent Republic of

Ireland, or Eire, and the six counties of Northern Ireland, or Ulster.

Dublin, originally founded by Vikings, is now a vibrant and truly cosmopolitan city while the proud city of Belfast is one of the jewels in the crown of Ulster.

It was Saint Patrick who first brought the light of Christianity to Ireland in the fifth century A.D.

Interpretations of this Christian message have varied over the centuries, often leading to bitter sectarian conflict – but the many intricately sculpted Celtic Crosses found all over the island are symbolic of a unity that crosses the sectarian divide.

It is an image that fuses the 'old gods' of the Celts with Christianity.

All the signs from the early years of this new millennium indicate that sectarian strife may soon become a thing of the past – with the Irish and their many kinsfolk across the world, be they Protestant or Catholic, finding common purpose in the rich tapestry of their shared heritage.

Chapter two:

Sons of the warrior

**The original Gaelic-Irish name of MacFhlannchaidh
was borne for centuries by the proud clan known more
familiarly today as Clancy.**

The name indicates 'son of the red haired warrior' – an
apt description for a clan that was involved from earliest
times in Ireland's turbulent history and whose rather
bloodthirsty crest features a hand holding a sword impaling
a boar's head.

What are now the counties of Sligo, Clare, and Leitrim
were the territories of the Clancys, with the Clancys of Co.
Clare settled in the area of the barony of Corcomroe and the
branch known as the Clancys of Dartry, in Leitrim, settled
in the barony of Rosclogher on the shores of Lough Melvin.

The ancestry of the Clancys is truly illustrious,
descended as they are from the tribal grouping known as the
Race of Cas, also known as the DalgCais, or Dalcassians.

The Dalcassians were named from the legendary
Cormac Cas, the early to mid-third century chieftain of the
province of Munster who was renowned for his remarkable
courage, strength, and dexterity.

It was Cormac Cas who inflicted a celebrated defeat on
the men of the province of Leinster in a battle fought near
present day Wexford, but was killed in battle in 254A.D. at

Dun-tri-Liag, or the Fort of the Stone Slabs, known today as Duntrileague, in Co. Limerick.

His deathblow, according to the ancient annals, came from the spear of the Leinster king known rather colourfully as Eochy of the Red Eyebrows.

It is from a descendant of Cormac Cas that the proud clan of the O'Briens take their name.

This was no less a figure than Brian Bóruma mac Cénnetig, a younger son of Cénnetig, king of Thomond, in the northern reaches of the province of Munster, and who was born about 926A.D.

Branches of the Clancys, as fellow Dalcassians, came to hold the honoured position of hereditary brehons, or lawyers, to the O'Briens – whose crest also features a hand holding a sword.

Involved in such close kinship with the O'Briens, the Clancys shared in both their glorious fortunes and tragic misfortunes.

Late tenth and early eleventh century Ireland was the scene of vicious inter-clan rivalry as successive clan chiefs fought for supremacy over their rivals, and it was this disunity that worked to the advantage of Viking invaders.

The period 795A.D. to 1014A.D. is known to Irish history as The Viking Tyranny, and it was largely through the inspired leadership of Brian Boru that Viking power was diminished, although not completely eliminated.

He was able to achieve this by managing to rally a

number of other chieftains to his cause – although by no means all.

With his battle-hardened warriors known as the Dalcassian knights at his side, Boru had by 1002A.D. achieved the prize of the High Kingship of Ireland – but there were still rival chieftains, and not least the Vikings, to deal with.

These Vikings, known as Ostmen, had occupied and fortified Dublin in the mid-ninth century and had other important trading settlements in other parts of the island.

Resenting Boru's High Kingship, a number of chieftains, particularly those of the province of Leinster, found common cause with the Ostmen, and the two sides met in final and bloody confrontation at the battle of Clontarf, four miles north of Dublin, on Good Friday 1014.

Boru proved victorious, but the annals speak of great slaughter on the day, with the dead piled high on the field of battle.

Among the many dead were Brian Boru's three sons, while he was killed by a party of fleeing Vikings, but not before felling most of them with his great two-handed sword.

His descendants rapidly consolidated their power base in Thomond, ruling there for centuries as kings and princes of Thomond and amassing other honours and titles along the way.

The O'Briens split into various branches, but the

Clancys of Co. Clare continued as their hereditary brehons.

The territorial map of the native Irish clans changed forever in the wake of the Norman invasion of the island in the late twelfth century and the subsequent consolidation of the power of the English Crown.

The map now showed three 'separate' Irelands.

These were the territories of privileged and powerful Anglo-Norman adventurers; the Ireland of the disaffected Gaelic-Irish such as the Clancys, who held lands unoccupied by the Normans - and the Pale, comprised of Dublin itself and a substantial area of its environs ruled over by an English elite.

What had been created was a highly volatile powder keg of grievances whose fuse would be periodically lit in the form of rebellions that would stain the soil of the Emerald Isle red with blood.

One graphic illustration of the conditions that sparked off rebellion by the native Irish clans can be found in a desperate plea sent to Pope John XII by Roderick O'Carroll of Ely, Donald O'Neil of Ulster, and a number of other Irish chieftains as early as 1318.

They stated: 'As it very constantly happens, whenever an Englishman, by perfidy or craft, kills an Irishman, however noble, or however innocent, be he clergy or layman, there is no penalty or correction enforced against the person who may be guilty of such wicked murder.

'But rather the more eminent the person killed and the

higher rank which he holds among his own people, so much more is the murderer honoured and rewarded by the English, and not merely by the people at large, but also by the religious and bishops of the English race.'

The Pope, perhaps unsurprisingly, was powerless to curb this harsh treatment.

Matters were exacerbated when a policy of 'plantation', or settlement of loyal Protestants on land held by native Irish such as the Clancys was put into effect during the reign from 1491 to 1547 of Henry VIII, whose Reformation effectively outlawed the established Roman Catholic faith throughout his dominions.

This plantation continued throughout the subsequent reigns of Elizabeth I, James I (James VI of Scotland), and in the wake of the Cromwellian invasion of 1649.

Many native Irish clans adopted the view that any enemy of England was their friend, and this explains why the Clancys and others gave aid to shipwrecked survivors of the Spanish Armada in September of 1588.

The 130-strong Spanish fleet, intent on the invasion of England, was scattered in heavy storms after its defeat at the battle of Gravelines, and many vessels were driven towards the west coast of Ireland.

This caused alarm on the part of the English authorities on the island, who feared, not without justification, that the disaffected native Irish would rally to their rescue.

William Fitzwilliam, Lord Deputy of Ireland, even

sanctioned the use of torture against survivors, while also ordering that anyone who came to their aid would be declared traitors.

At least 24 Spanish vessels are believed to have been wrecked on the Irish coastline – from Co. Antrim in the north of the island to Co. Kerry in the south.

It was not until the late nineteenth century that a curious document was unearthed in the archives of the Academia de la Historia in Madrid.

It had been written by Don Francisco de Cuellar, who related how he had been rescued by the Clancys and afforded shelter and hospitality – at great risk to themselves – at Rosclogher, on the shores of Lough Melvin.

Chapter three:
Flight of the Wild Geese

Following the devastations that came in the wake of the invasion of Ireland in 1649 of England's 'Lord Protector' Oliver Cromwell, the final death knell of the ancient Gaelic order of proud native Irish clans such as the Clancys was sounded.

This was in the form of what is known in Ireland as Cogadh an Dá Rí, or The War of the Two Kings.

Also known as the Williamite War in Ireland or the Jacobite War in Ireland, it was sparked off in 1688 when the Stuart monarch James II (James VII of Scotland) was deposed and fled into exile in France.

The Protestant William of Orange and his wife Mary were invited to take up the thrones of Scotland, Ireland, and England – but James still had significant support in Ireland, with his supporters known as Jacobites.

Following the arrival in England of William and Mary from Holland, Richard Talbot, 1st Earl of Tyrconnell and James's Lord Deputy in Ireland, assembled an army loyal to the Stuart cause.

The aim was to garrison and fortify the island in the name of James and quell any resistance.

Londonderry, or Derry, proved loyal to the cause of William of Orange, or William III as he had become, and managed to hold out against a siege that was not lifted until July 28, 1689.

James, with the support of troops and money supplied by Louis XIV of France, had landed at Kinsale in March of 1689 and joined forces with his Irish supporters.

A series of military encounters followed, culminating in James's defeat by an army commanded by William at the battle of the Boyne on July 12, 1689.

James again fled into French exile, never to return, while another significant Jacobite defeat occurred in July of 1691 at the battle of Aughrim – with about half their army killed on the field, wounded, or taken prisoner.

The Williamite forces then besieged Limerick and the Jacobites were forced into surrender in September of 1691.

A peace treaty, known as the Treaty of Limerick followed, under which those Jacobites willing to swear an oath of loyalty to William were allowed to remain in their native land.

Those reluctant to do so, including many native Irish such as the Clancys, were allowed to seek exile on foreign shores, where they joined the military service of both France and Spain – England's enemies.

This departure of native Irish to fight for the cause of England's enemies had first started in the sixteenth century and continued up until the eighteenth century.

Known as The Flight of the Wild Geese, it was a process that saw the formation of famed Irish Brigades, and it was in the ranks of these brigades that many Clancys gained distinction – particularly in the service of Spain.

Clancys had been among the disillusioned and weary ranks of the defeated Jacobite army that departed Ireland for French shores under the command of Patrick Sarsfield in October of 1691, while some had been among 1300 former rebel soldiers who were deported from Ireland in 1609 by Arthur Chichester, Lord Deputy of Ireland, to serve in the Swedish Army.

Sweden was England's ally, and many of the soldiers promptly defected to enter the military service of Spain.

A further flight abroad of native Irish such as the Clancys came in 1789 in the wake of the abortive Rising of that year.

The roots of the Rising are tangled in the thick undergrowth of Irish history, but in essence it was sparked off by a fusion of sectarian and agrarian unrest and a burning desire for political reform that had been shaped by the French revolutionary slogan of 'liberty, equality, and fraternity.'

A movement had come into existence that embraced middle-class intellectuals and the oppressed peasantry, and if this loosely bound movement could be said to have a leader, it was Wolfe Tone, a Protestant from Kildare and leading light of a radical republican movement known as the United Irishmen.

Despite attempts by the British government to concede a degree of agrarian and political reform, it was a case of far too little and much too late, and by 1795 the United Irishmen, through Wolfe Tone, was receiving help from France.

A French invasion fleet was despatched to Ireland in December of 1796, but it was scattered by storms off Bantry Bay.

Two years later, in the summer of 1798, rebellion broke out on the island.

The first flames of revolt were fanned in Ulster, but soon died out, only to be replaced by a much more serious conflagration centred mainly in Co. Wexford.

Victory was achieved at the battle of Oulart Hill, followed by another victory at the battle of Three Rocks, but the peasant army was no match for the 20,000 troops or so that descended on Wexford.

Defeat followed at the battle of Vinegar Hill on 21 June, followed by another decisive defeat at Kilcumney Hill five days later.

The Rising of 1798 at last came to an end, while the authorities executed Wolfe Tone after a botched suicide attempt.

Two years later, the parliaments of Ireland and Britain were united in an Act of Union and movements immediately sprang up for its repeal.

Among the most vociferous opponents of the union and a leading campaigner for Home Rule was John Joseph Clancy, more familiarly known as the Irish Nationalist politician J. J.Clancy.

The life and times of this distinguished bearer of the Clancy name are in many ways mirror reflections of one of the most crucial periods in Irish history.

Born in 1847 in Annaghdown, Co. Galway, and the son of a farmer, he had gained a degree in Ancient Classics from Queen's College, Galway, by the time he was aged 22, and two years later found himself on the editorial staff of the Irish Nationalist weekly newspaper *The Nation*.

Later promoted to the editorship of the paper, he also found time to become involved in a host of nationalist organisations such as the Home Rule League, the Young Ireland Society, the Land League, the Irish Labour and Industrial Union, and the Irish National League.

Not only a talented writer but also a gifted orator, he was elected as an Irish Nationalist Member of Parliament (M.P.) for the British House of Commons in 1885 and, a year later, to the post of editor of the Irish Press Agency in London.

A staunch supporter of the ill-starred Nationalist leader Charles Stewart Parnell, Clancy defended him in the bitter row that erupted both in the House of Commons and in Ireland itself over Parnell's love affair with Kitty O'Shea.

Parnell died a broken man in October of 1891 but Clancy, along with fellow politicians such as John Redmond, were among a minority, known as Parnellites, who kept his memory alive.

Years of frustration followed until the Home Rule Act

finally received its royal assent in September of 1914, but Clancy had used the intervening time to great effect.

Still functioning as an M.P., he was responsible for a number of important measures that greatly benefited the ordinary folk of his native land.

These included the framing of various land acts that allowed tenants to buy their holdings, the introduction of democratic local government, restoration of the right of workers to strike and, through the Housing Act of 1908, a radical improvement in housing conditions.

It was also through the efforts of the tireless Clancy that today's National University of Ireland was established, effectively removing barriers that had previously existed to Roman Catholics receiving higher education.

He continued active in politics until his death in 1928.

Yet another John Joseph Clancy also played a prominent role in early twentieth century Irish politics.

Born in 1891, he was a Sinn Fein member of the First Dáil, or Irish Parliament, for Sligo North from between 1918 and 1921.

Later serving as an officer in the Irish Free State Army, he was imprisoned on several occasions and died in 1932.

Peadar Clancy, born in Co. Clare in 1888, played a role in the abortive Easter Rising of 1916, serving the republican cause in what was known as the Four Courts Garrison.

As the bitter struggle for Irish independence from British rule intensified, the Irish Citizen Army (I.C.A.) had joined forces with the Irish Republican Brotherhood (I.R.B.) to mount the Rising, known in Irish as Éiri Amach na Cásca, following a proclamation of independence signed by James Connolly and six others.

With Connolly as Commandant of the Dublin Brigade, the aim was to wrest independence from Britain by force of arms and, accordingly, on April 24, Easter Monday, the combined republican forces of the I.C.A. and the I.R.B. seized strategic locations throughout Dublin, including the General Post Office.

Other Risings were timed to take place simultaneously throughout the counties of Galway, Wexford, and Louth.

With a force of less than 5,000 republicans matched against no less than 16,000 well armed and trained troops and 1,000 armed police, the Rising was doomed to failure – coming to a bloody and exhausted conclusion on April 30th after its leaders were forced into reluctant surrender.

More than 1,200 republicans, troops, police, and civilians had been killed, but further deaths followed as the sixteen leaders of the Rising, including Connolly, were executed by the British Crown in Dublin's Kilmainham Jail.

Four years after the Rising, in November of 1920, Clancy and two fellow republicans were killed by their captors while imprisoned in Dublin Castle in circumstances that remain controversially unclear to this day.

Chapter four:

On the world stage

Far from civil strife, bearers of the name of Clancy have excelled, and continue to excel, in a wide range of endeavours.

A master of the political thriller, **Tom Clancy** is the best-selling American author who was born in 1947 in Calvert County, Maryland.

Renowned for his attention to highly technical military and scientific detail, his rather unlikely career before he turned his talents to writing was running an independent insurance company.

He came to international attention and acclaim in 1984 with the publication of his first novel, *The Hunt for Red October*, adapted for the screen six years later and starring Sean Connery and Alec Baldwin.

His 1987 *Patriot Games* was also adapted for the screen, starring Harrison Ford, while other novels include *The Cardinal of the Kremlin*, *Rainbow Six*, and *Without Remorse*.

The Tom Clancy name is also used as a 'brand' for similar novels written by other writers.

Away from writing, he is also part owner of the American Major League Baseball team the Baltimore Orioles.

In the world of music **The Clancy Brothers** are

recognised as having been among the first to popularise Irish traditional music, bringing it to an international audience.

Particularly popular throughout the 1960s, the band had various line-ups, but the core members were the brothers Paddy, Tom, Bobby, and Liam Clancy, along with fellow Irish musician Tommy Makem.

Paddy and Tom, the oldest brothers, born in Carrick-on-Suir, in Co. Tipperary, left their homeland for Canada after serving in the Second World War, but by 1949 they had settled in New York.

The two brothers quickly made names for themselves as Broadway actors, but later turned to music.

They were subsequently joined by their other brothers and Tommy Makem, although Bobby Clancy returned to Ireland for a time.

Their popularity soon grew to such an extent that they appeared live on America's Ed Sullivan Show in March of 1961, to a television audience of 80 million people.

It was before appearing on the Sullivan show that their mother back home in Ireland sent them white Irish-knit Aran sweaters, and these became their trademark.

The Clancy Brothers, along with Tommy Makem, also appeared live at the prestigious venue of New York's Carnegie Hall, while albums released by them include the 1955 *The Lark in the Morning*, *The Rising of the Moon*, and the 1961 *The Clancy Brothers and Tommy Makem*.

Tom Clancy died in 1990 at the age of 66, while brother

Paddy died in 1998, aged 76, and Bobby in 2002, aged 75.

The only surviving brother is Liam, who was born in 1935, while Tommy Makem died in 2007.

Also in the field of traditional Irish music **Willie Clancy**, born in 1918 in Miltown, Malbay, in Co. Clare, and who died in 1973, was a renowned practitioner of the Irish uilleann pipes, an instrument he first took up in his late teens after mastering the whistle and the flute.

Clancys have also excelled and continue to excel in the competitive arena of sport.

Inducted into the Hockey Hall of Fame and Canada's Sport Hall of Fame, Francis Clancy, born in Ottawa in 1903, was better known to ice hockey fans as **King Clancy**.

The nickname originated from his father, who played football for Ottawa, and was dubbed 'King' Clancy – but Frank soon became 'king' of ice hockey as a player, coach, referee, and team executive.

As a defenceman he played sixteen games in the National Hockey League for the Ottawa Senators and Toronto Maple Leafs. He died in 1986.

The King Clancy Memorial trophy, awarded annually to the hockey player who, by example, demonstrates qualities of leadership on and off the ice and who has made exceptional humanitarian contributions in the community, is named in his honour.

His son **Terry Clancy**, born in Ottawa in 1943, is the retired ice hockey player who played 93 games in the

National Hockey League, playing for teams that included the Oakland Seals and the Toronto Maple Leafs.

In baseball **John Clancy**, born in 1900 in Odell, Illinois, and who died in 1968, was a noted American first baseman in Major League Baseball from 1924 to 1934, while **James Clancy**, born in 1955 in Chicago, is a former starting pitcher in Major League.

Teams he played for include the Toronto Blue Jays, Houston Astros, and Atlanta Braves.

In European football **Tim Clancy**, born in 1984, is the Irish full-back who, at the time of writing, plays for Kilmarnock in the Scottish Premier League after having played for teams that include Celtic and Millwall.

In American football **John Clancy**, born in Humboldt, Iowa, in 1944, is the former wide receiver who played for the Miami Dolphins in 1967 and 1969 and the Green Bay Packers in 1970.

A lingerie and catwalk model, **Abigail Clancy**, born in 1986 in Liverpool, is best known as the celebrity girlfriend of England football star Peter Crouch.

Her brother **Kyle Clancy** is a professional footballer who, at the time of writing, plays for Blackpool, while her brother **Sean Clancy** plays for Conference North club Burscough.

On the cycle track **Ed Clancy**, born in 1985, is the British professional track and road bicycle racer who won the first stage of the 2005 Tour of Berlin and the 2007 Team Pursuit World Championship.

He was also part of the British team that set a new world record in the 2008 Team Pursuit World Championship.

In the world of politics **Mary Clancy**, born in 1948 in Halifax, Nova Scotia, served as a member of the Canadian House of Commons from 1988 to 1997, representing Halifax.

Following her term in Parliament she served until 2004 as Canadian Consul General to Boston.

In American politics **Donald D. Clancy**, born in Cincinnati in 1921 and who died in 2007, was the distinguished Republican Congressman who represented the 2nd District of Ohio from 1961 to 1971, having served as Mayor of Cincinnati from 1958 until 1960.

Born in Detroit in 1892, **Robert Clancy** was the former journalist and lawyer who served as secretary to the Assistant United States Secretary of Commerce from 1913 to 1917.

He served as manager of America's War Trade Board at Detroit during the First World War, and later served as Democrat Congressman for Michigan until the early 1930s. He died in 1962.

Clancys have also literally put their name on the American landscape – with Clancy the name of a community in Jefferson County, Montana.

Key dates in Ireland's history from the first settlers to the formation of the Irish Republic:

circa 7000 B.C. Arrival and settlement of Stone Age
                    people.
circa 3000 B.C. Arrival of settlers of New Stone Age
                    period.
circa 600 B.C. First arrival of the Celts.
200 A.D.   Establishment of Hill of Tara, Co. Meath,
                    as seat of the High Kings.
circa 432 A.D. Christian mission of St. Patrick.
800-920 A.D.   Invasion and subsequent settlement of
                    Vikings.
1002 A.D.   Brian Boru recognised as High King.
1014   Brian Boru killed at battle of Clontarf.
1169-1170   Cambro-Norman invasion of the island.
1171   Henry II claims Ireland for the English
                    Crown.
1366   Statutes of Kilkenny ban marriage
                    between native Irish and English.
1529-1536   England's Henry VIII embarks on
                    religious Reformation.
1536   Earl of Kildare rebels against the Crown.
1541   Henry VIII declared King of Ireland.
1558   Accession to English throne of Elizabeth I.
1565   Battle of Affane.
1569-1573   First Desmond Rebellion.
1579-1583   Second Desmond Rebellion.
1594-1603   Nine Years War.
1606   Plantation' of Scottish and English settlers.

1607	Flight of the Earls.
1632-1636	Annals of the Four Masters compiled.
1641	Rebellion over policy of plantation and other grievances.
1649	Beginning of Cromwellian conquest.
1688	Flight into exile in France of Catholic Stuart monarch James II as Protestant Prince William of Orange invited to take throne of England along with his wife, Mary.
1689	William and Mary enthroned as joint monarchs; siege of Derry.
1690	Jacobite forces of James defeated by William at battle of the Boyne (July) and Dublin taken.
1691	Athlone taken by William; Jacobite defeats follow at Aughrim, Galway, and Limerick; conflict ends with Treaty of Limerick (October) and Irish officers allowed to leave for France.
1695	Penal laws introduced to restrict rights of Catholics; banishment of Catholic clergy.
1704	Laws introduced constricting rights of Catholics in landholding and public office.
1728	Franchise removed from Catholics.
1791	Foundation of United Irishmen republican movement.
1796	French invasion force lands in Bantry Bay.
1798	Defeat of Rising in Wexford and death of United Irishmen leaders Wolfe Tone and Lord Edward Fitzgerald.

1800	Act of Union between England and Ireland.
1803	Dublin Rising under Robert Emmet.
1829	Catholics allowed to sit in Parliament.
1845-1849	The Great Hunger: thousands starve to death as potato crop fails and thousands more emigrate.
1856	Phoenix Society founded.
1858	Irish Republican Brotherhood established.
1873	Foundation of Home Rule League.
1893	Foundation of Gaelic League.
1904	Foundation of Irish Reform Association.
1913	Dublin strikes and lockout.
1916	Easter Rising in Dublin and proclamation of an Irish Republic.
1917	Irish Parliament formed after Sinn Fein election victory.
1919-1921	War between Irish Republican Army and British Army.
1922	Irish Free State founded, while six northern counties remain part of United Kingdom as Northern Ireland, or Ulster; civil war up until 1923 between rival republican groups.
1949	Foundation of Irish Republic after all remaining constitutional links with Britain are severed.